D1708883

Lerner SPORTS

BEHIND THE SCENES

GYMNASTICS

by Blythe Lawrence

Lerner Publications ◆ Minneapolis

Lerner Publications Company
A division of Lerner Publishing Group, Inc.
241 First Avenue North
Minneapolis, MN 55401 USA

For reading levels and more information, look up this title at *www.lernerbooks.com*.

The images in this book are used with the permission of: © Karim Jaafar/AFP/Getty Images, p. 1; © Petr Toman/Shutterstock.com, pp. 4–5; © Laurence Griffiths/Getty Images Sport/Getty Images, p. 6; © Cheriss May/NurPhoto/Getty Images, p. 7; © oleg66/Getty Images, pp. 8–9; © Image Source/Getty Images, pp. 10–11; © Jared Wickerham/Getty Images Sport/Getty Images, p. 12; © Andy Buchanan/AFP/Getty Images, p. 13; © David Eulitt/Kansas City Star/MCT/Tribune News Service/Getty Images, pp. 14–15; © Barry Chin/The Boston Globe/Getty Images, p. 16; © Ben Radford/Corbis/Corbis Sport/Getty Images, p. 18; © Ulrik Pedersen/NurPhoto/Getty Images, p. 19; © Tim Clayton/Corbis/Corbis Sport/Getty Images, pp. 20–21; © BSIP/UIG/Universal Images Group/Getty Images, p. 22; © David Livingston/Getty Images Entertainment/Getty Images, p. 24–25; © Todd Williamson/Amazon/Getty Images Entertainment/Getty Images, pp. 26–27; © Sergey Novikov/Shutterstock.com, p. 29.

Front cover: © Karim Jaafar/AFP/Getty Images.

Main body text set in Myriad Pro.
Typeface provided by Adobe.

Library of Congress Cataloging-in-Publication Data

Names: Lawrence, Blythe, author.
Title: Behind the scenes gymnastics / Blythe Lawrence.
Description: Minneapolis : Lerner Publications, [2020] | Series: Inside the sport | Includes bibliographical references and index. | Audience: Ages: 7–11. | Audience: Grades: 4–6.
Identifiers: LCCN 2018050534 (print) | LCCN 2019004535 (ebook) | ISBN 9781541556294 (eb pdf) | ISBN 9781541556089 (lb : alk. paper) | ISBN 9781541574373 (pb : alk. paper)
Subjects: LCSH: Gymnasts—Juvenile literature. | Gymnastics—Training—Juvenile literature. | Gymnastics—Training. sears
Classification: LCC GV461.3 (ebook) | LCC GV461.3 .L38 2020 (print) | DDC 796.44—dc23

LC record available at *https://lccn.loc.gov/2018050534*

Manufactured in the United States of America
2-48604-43480-10/10/2019

CONTENTS

GOLD MEDALS

Simone Biles stood at the edge of the spring floor. She tried not to look at the Olympic rings. The nineteen-year-old gymnast still could not believe she was actually at the 2016 Olympic Games. She was about to compete in the last event of the women's gymnastics team final.

Biles had dreamed of this for many years. She had practiced for thousands of hours. In this moment she just had to perform one more great floor routine. Then the US women's team would be Olympic gold medalists.

Simone Biles's outstanding score on the floor exercise was needed for Team USA to win the Olympic gold medal. ▶

FACTS
at a Glance

- Female gymnasts compete in four events: vault, uneven bars, balance beam, and floor exercise. Men compete in six events: floor exercise, pommel horse, still rings, vault, parallel bars, and high bar.

- Many gymnasts start practicing at a young age.

- Gymnasts train a lot to perfect their routines. The top gymnasts may spend up to forty hours per week preparing before major competitions.

- Gymnasts connect with fans through social media, master classes, and volunteer work.

Simone Biles, left, stands with other members of Team USA to celebrate their gold medals.
▼

An Olympic gold medal from
◀ the 2016 Summer Olympic
Games in Rio de Janeiro, Brazil

The judges watched Biles. She raised her arms to show that she was ready to perform. She calmly stepped onto the mat. Music filled the arena. Biles moved to the music. She performed tumbling passes from one corner of the mat to the other. Between the passes, she did leaps, jumps, and dance moves.

Biles finished ninety seconds later. The arena burst into applause. Biles waved and ran off the floor. She did it! Her flawless routine clinched the gold medal for her team. Two nights later, Biles gave another performance in the individual all-around final to win a second gold medal all on her own.

How did Biles and her teammates make it to the Olympics? Their gold medals came after years of training, hard work, and practice.

CHAPTER 1

THE PATH TO THE OLYMPICS

Most Olympic gymnasts started practicing when they were very young. Many started when they were four or five years old. But some started when they were older. US national champion Yul Moldauer didn't set foot in a gym until he was almost eight.

Gymnasts start in beginner classes. Their coaches introduce the different gymnastics events. Women compete in four events: vault, uneven bars, balance beam, and floor exercise. Men do six events: floor exercise, pommel horse, still rings, vault, parallel bars, and high bar.

Even at a young age, gymnasts have to practice a lot if they want to be great. ▶

USA

The best young
gymnasts might get
noticed by the US
national team.

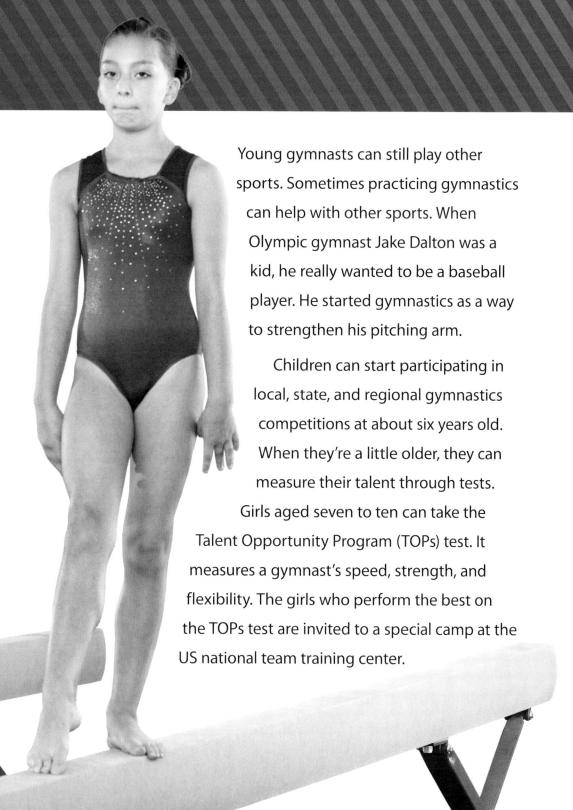

Young gymnasts can still play other sports. Sometimes practicing gymnastics can help with other sports. When Olympic gymnast Jake Dalton was a kid, he really wanted to be a baseball player. He started gymnastics as a way to strengthen his pitching arm.

Children can start participating in local, state, and regional gymnastics competitions at about six years old. When they're a little older, they can measure their talent through tests. Girls aged seven to ten can take the Talent Opportunity Program (TOPs) test. It measures a gymnast's speed, strength, and flexibility. The girls who perform the best on the TOPs test are invited to a special camp at the US national team training center.

Elite gymnast Kyla Ross competes on the uneven bars at the 2014 US Gymnastics Championships.

There, they may learn from national team coaches. Young male gymnasts can also take a test to attend a similar camp. Coaches look for future stars at these camps.

It takes gymnasts years to master complicated skills and routines. Some young gymnasts practice after school almost every day. Many eventually drop other activities to focus on only gymnastics.

Gymnasts are assigned a level for competition that matches their skill level. The levels range from 1 to 10. Gymnasts must perfect skills at each level to move up to the next level. Each level gets harder. Gymnasts usually spend more time practicing when they get to the higher levels. The best gymnasts reach higher than level 10. They are called elite gymnasts.

Not many gymnasts make it to the elite level. Only elites compete at the US Gymnastics Championships. The best at the championships are picked to be part of the US national team. That team represents the United States at worldwide competitions, including the Olympic Games.

Russian gymnast Irina Alekseeva competes on the balance beam.
▼

CHAPTER 2

COMPETITION DAY

Most gymnasts are excited and nervous before a big competition. They do all they can to make sure they are ready to perform their routines. This starts with eating a good meal the night before. The meal might have meat or pasta. Then gymnasts eat a light, healthful breakfast the morning of the competition. These foods give gymnasts plenty of energy.

Since competitions can last for hours, many gymnasts pack snacks and drinks in their gym bags. The gym bag has everything a gymnast needs. This includes special shoes for floor and vault events, hand grips for bars, and a competition uniform.

Elite gymnast Aly Raisman uses hand grips to compete on the uneven bars. ▶

Gymnasts stretch and practice their routines before a competition.

At the arena, it's time to warm up. Competitors stretch out on the floor. They do handstands and basic moves to warm up their bodies. They're usually quiet. They think about the competition to come.

After the warmup, groups rotate to practice on equipment for each event. They spend fifteen to twenty minutes doing parts of their routines and getting used to the equipment. This practice is important because the equipment in a competition arena may feel different than the equipment the gymnasts train on at home. If gymnasts have traveled a long way to a competition, they may have a day or two to practice in the arena before competition day.

Gymnasts return to the locker room before the competition to change clothes. Women normally compete in long-sleeved leotards. Men wear unitards and shorts or long pants, depending on the event. Gymnasts with long hair make sure it's pulled back, away from their faces. As the competition begins, teams march out single file to be introduced to the crowd. The crowd cheers.

Before starting a routine, a gymnast stands beside the equipment. He waits for a green light or green flag from the judge. When the judge gives the signal, the gymnast has thirty seconds to begin the routine.

Stats Spotlight
44

That's the number of years between male gymnasts winning back-to-back Olympic medals in the men's all-around competition. At the 2016 Olympic Games in Brazil, gymnast Kohei Uchimura of Japan won a medal in the all-around competition at his second Olympics in a row. Japan's Sawao Kato was the last to do so, winning gold in 1968 and 1972.

Gymnasts are very focused during their routines. They put all of their energy into performing as perfectly as possible. Gymnasts pay extra close attention to the ending of their routines because that is the last thing the judges see.

After the competition, winners are honored in an awards ceremony. Then the gymnasts talk to reporters. At the World Championships or Olympic Games, reporters are invited into a room where the gymnasts sit at a table with microphones to answer questions.

▲
John Orozco of Team USA stays focused as he performs a routine on the pommel horse.

Sam Mikulak of Team USA competes on the parallel bars in 2018.

After that, the gymnasts are free to go. When they leave they may be stopped by fans eager to take their photo or congratulate them. For some gymnasts, this is one of the best parts of the day.

CHAPTER 3

WORKING OUT

When preparing for the World Championships or Olympic Games, elite gymnasts may spend up to forty hours per week in the gym. That's the same as having a full-time job. Workouts often happen twice a day for three to four hours at a time. During this time, gymnasts practice their routines. They also stretch and exercise to strengthen their muscles.

Gymnasts practice their routines over and over. They want the routines to be perfect for competition. They also spend a lot of time practicing moves separately to build their strength.

Olympic gymnast McKayla Maroney prepares during a training session before the 2013 US Gymnastics Championships. ▶

A young gymnast practices with a trampoline and a pit of foam blocks.

Practicing so much is hard on gymnasts' bodies. Sometimes their muscles and joints hurt. Some gymnasts work with special trainers who massage their muscles. They also might do special exercises to strengthen a weak muscle or to rebuild strength after an injury. US national champion Sam Mikulak likes spending time in a steam room after his workouts. Others soak in hot or cold water. Some put ice on sore muscles.

Gymnasts need a lot of energy for their hard workouts. They need to eat well so they can perform well. Some gymnasts work with professional nutritionists to plan healthful meals.

Gymnasts practice with a lot of different equipment. Trampolines give gymnasts extra spring to practice new tumbling and vaulting skills. Pits filled with foam blocks provide a soft surface to fall into.

Many gyms have a spotting belt. This is a belt connected to a cord that lifts the gymnast into the air. Coaches help gymnasts use spotting belts. This can make it easier for gymnasts to learn new moves in the air.

The competition season for elite gymnasts starts with World Cup events in the spring and ends with the World Championships in the fall. During an Olympic year, there are no World Championships. The season ends in late summer with the Olympic Games. Because there are no competitions in the winter, winter workouts may be more relaxed. Gymnasts use that time to recover, work on new skills, and put together routines for the next year.

Stats Spotlight

7

That's the number of Olympic Games in which Oksana Chusovitina has competed. As of 2016, she had competed in every summer Olympics since 1992. She was the only elite gymnast in the world older than forty, and she had no plans to stop competing.

CHAPTER 4

LIFE OUTSIDE THE GYM

After their Olympic wins, Simone Biles and her teammates took time off to have fun. They toured the country performing a gymnastics show. Biles got to walk on celebrity red carpets and was honored at events. She was on the reality TV show *Dancing with the Stars.*

Social media allows gymnasts to connect with their fans. Many use Twitter and Instagram accounts to show their lives outside the gym. They post videos of new routines and funny things that happen in training. In the summer, gymnasts also connect with fans by appearing at gym camps or hosting master classes.

#DWTS

Simone Biles and her *Dancing with the Stars* partner Sasha Farber ▶

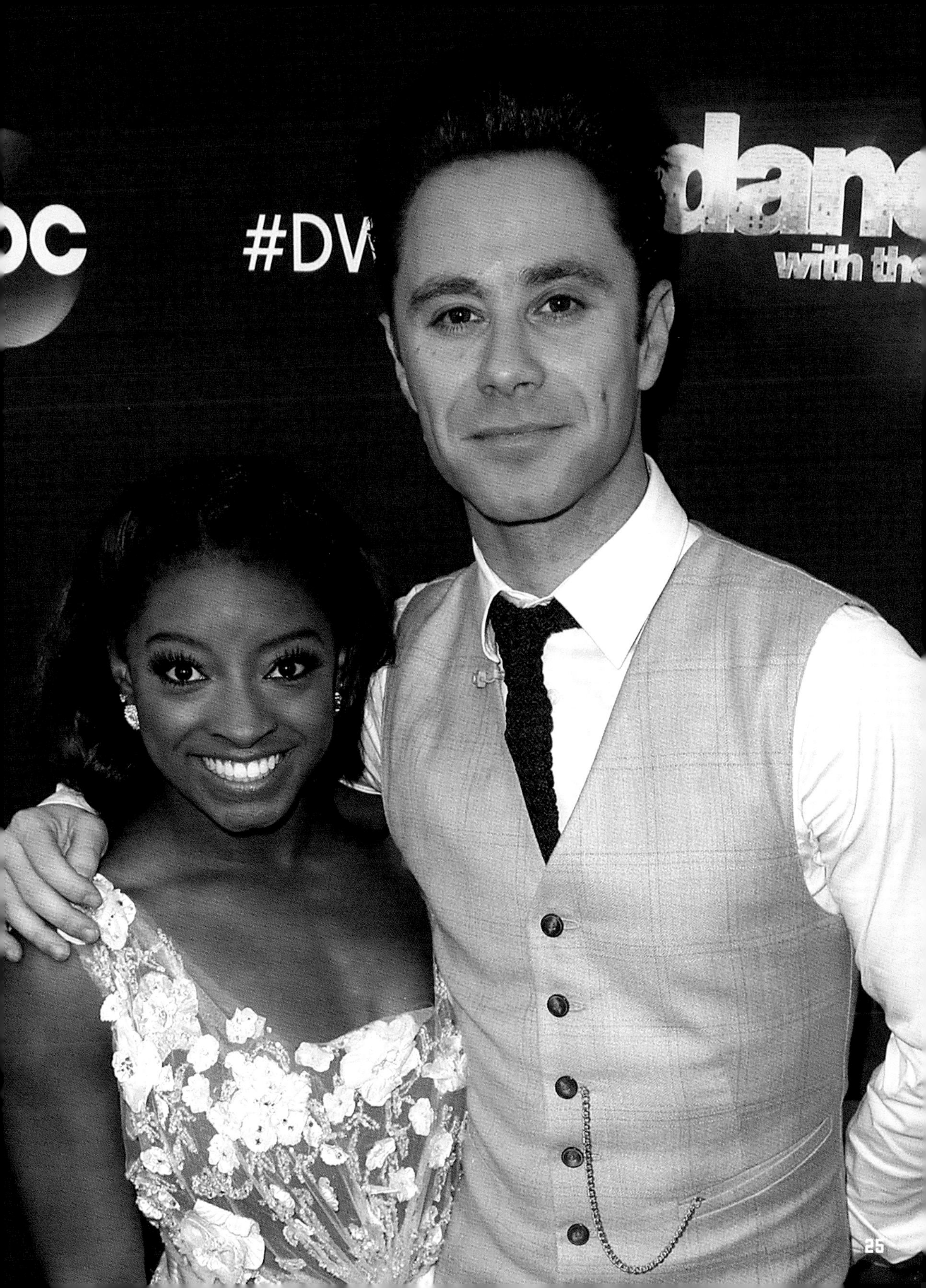
#DW
with th

Some gymnasts volunteer with groups they care about. Olympic gold medalist Laurie Hernandez worked with Orgullosa, a group that supports Latina women.

Most elite men's gymnasts are in their late teens or twenties. Many have completed college. But most elite women are teenagers. They spend so much time training that sometimes they are not able to have typical high school experiences. Many are homeschooled or take online classes. Some miss out on events like proms and football games.

But gymnasts feel their sport is very rewarding. Gymnastics helps them feel confident and strong. Olympic gymnasts continue to impress fans and inspire young gymnasts to work hard. Someday they may win Olympic gold too!

▲
Olympic gymnast Laurie Hernandez
meets with young gymnasts at the
Los Angeles School of Gymnastics.

YOUR TURN

A straight handstand is one of the most basic moves in gymnastics. The best gymnasts can hold a handstand for several minutes. The skill is not difficult to master, but it takes practice. Follow these steps to do a handstand. Ask an adult to watch you to make sure you don't fall.

Start in a standing position. Move one leg slightly in front of the other until your legs are shoulder-width apart. Bend your front knee slightly while keeping your foot on the ground. Keep your back leg straight. Raise your arms over your head so your elbows cover your ears. This is called a lunge position.

Lower your hands to touch the ground, keeping your chin to your chest. As your hands touch the ground, kick your back leg into the air and push off your front leg. Try to touch your legs together in the air. Keep your arms straight.

Anyone can practice a handstand at home. Friends can practice together.

Repeat the movement in reverse as you come down. The foot you pushed off with should touch the ground first, followed by your back leg.

You can first try doing the handstand against a wall to support you. Remember, practice makes perfect!

GLOSSARY

all-around
a competition in which scores from several events are added up to give a total. The gymnast with the highest total is the all-around champion.

elite
the highest level

focus
to concentrate

master classes
special classes taught by a famous gymnast

pommel horse
a leather-bound, bench-like object with handles in the middle. Male gymnasts perform routines while holding the handles and not letting their feet touch the ground.

spring floor
a floor exercise mat with springs under it that gives added bounce as gymnasts tumble on it

trainers
professionals who help people improve their physical fitness

tumbling passes
gymnastics skills such as somersaults and handsprings done in a row

vault
an event in which a gymnast runs down a runway, bounds off a springboard, and flies over a raised platform called a vault doing flips and twists

FURTHER
INFORMATION

FloGymnastics
www.flogymnastics.com

Hernandez, Laurie. *I Got This: To Gold and Beyond*. New York: HarperCollins
    Publishers, 2017.

International Gymnastics Federation
http://www.gymnastics.sport/site/index.php

Raisman, Aly with Blythe Lawrence. *Fierce: How Competing for Myself Changed
    Everything*. New York: Little, Brown and Company, 2017.

USA Gymnastics
www.usagym.org

INDEX

ABOUT THE AUTHOR

Blythe Lawrence is a journalist from Seattle, Washington.